599.8   Harman, Amanda.
HAR
           South American
           monkeys.

                                    YPVA34492

$21.36

DATE			
4-H '98			
MR 27 '98			
Ryan 312			
NO 04 '98			
240			
AP 14 '99			
6/30/04 A. Rose Sum Lot			

ENDANGERED!

SOUTH AMERICAN MONKEYS

Amanda Harman

Series Consultant: James G. Doherty
General Curator, The Bronx Zoo, New York

BENCHMARK BOOKS

MARSHALL CAVENDISH

NEW YORK

Benchmark Books
Marshall Cavendish Corporation
99 White Plains Road
Tarrytown, New York 10591-9001

©Marshall Cavendish Corporation, 1996

Library of Congress Cataloging-in-Publication Data

Harman, Amanda, 1968-
    South American monkeys / Amanda Harman.
        p.   cm. — (Endangered!)
    Includes bibliographical references (p.   ) and index.
    Summary: Introduces the monkeys of South America, many of which are now rare and endangered, such as the lion tamarin, woolly spider monkey, and bald uakari.
    ISBN 0-7614-0218-7 (library binding)
    1. Cebidae—South America—Juvenile literature.
2. Callitrichidae—South America—Juvenile literature. 3. Monkeys—South America—Juvenile literature. 4. Endangered species—South America—Juvenile literature. [1. Monkeys—South America. 2. Rare animals. 3. Endangered species.]   I. Title.   II. Series.
QL737.P925H38 1996
599.8'2'098—dc20   95-44806
                                                                        CIP
                                                                         AC

Printed in Hong Kong

PICTURE CREDITS
The publishers would like to thank the following picture libraries for supplying the photographs used in this book: Bruce Coleman 18, 19, 27, 29, BC; Frank Lane Picture Agency (FLPA) FC, 6, 8, 12, 13, 23; NHPA 1, 4, 5, 11, 21, 25; Oxford Scientific Films 9, 15, 17, 20, 22, 24, 28; Silvestris (via FLPA) 7, 14, 16, 26; Sunset (via FLPA) 10.

Series created by Brown Packaging

Front cover: Squirrel monkey.
Title page: Brown-headed spider monkey.
Back cover: Bald uakari.

Contents

Introduction

With their almost human faces and handlike front paws, monkeys often look like small, furry people. They are agile, curious, and full of mischief. People love to watch their antics, which can be very funny.

Monkeys – along with human beings and apes – are a special kind of **mammal** called a **primate**. Today South America has about 50 **species** of monkeys. There used to

There are two main types of monkeys: those that live in Africa and Asia, such as baboons and macaques, and monkeys that live in the Americas, like this bald uakari.

A black spider monkey peers down from its leafy perch high in the trees. Spider monkeys, the most agile South American monkeys, can move quickly and gracefully.

be more. Over the millions of years that monkeys have lived in the region, the climate and the plants and trees have changed. The species that could not **adapt** to these changes became **extinct**.

Sadly, many South American monkeys are now in danger of dying out. Today, however, they are threatened not by natural changes but by people. One of the main reasons monkeys are at risk is that their **rainforest** homes are being cut down. Without their familiar **habitats** and sources of food, monkeys cannot survive.

The different species of South American monkeys belong to a number of groups. In this book, we will look at five of these – marmosets and tamarins, spider monkeys, uakaris, squirrel monkeys, and woolly monkeys.

Marmosets and tamarins are the smallest South American monkeys. Since they are so light, they can scurry along the thinnest twigs high in the treetops. This is Geoffroy's tufted-ear marmoset.

Marmosets & Tamarins

The great **tropical** South American forests are home to the marmosets and tamarins. These monkeys also live in small patches of forest growing along the edges of rivers and streams. Marmosets and tamarins are active during the day and spend most of their time **foraging** for food. At least one third of their day is spent searching for small animals, such as spiders, insects, frogs, lizards, and snails.

Marmosets and tamarins have very long hands and fingers, which they use to reach into small holes and clumps of leaves for their **prey**. The rest of the time they feed on small, juicy buds, fruits, and flowers. Marmosets, but not tamarins, also like to drink tree **gum**. They do this by gouging holes in the tree trunks with the long teeth in their lower jaw. The marmosets then lick up the gum as it trickles out of the hole.

Marmosets and tamarins are very sociable monkeys. They live in large family groups of up to 15 animals, made up of one breeding pair and their young of various ages. The breeding female may have twins twice a year. When the babies are born, they are completely helpless for the first two weeks. The older offspring and the father take turns to help the mother carry them around. The rest of the

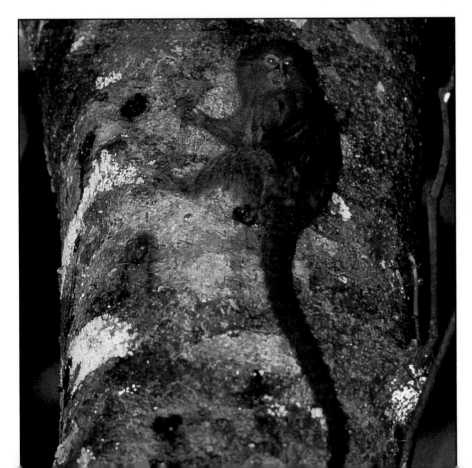

The pygmy marmoset is the tiniest monkey in the world! It is only about 15 inches (38 cm) long including its tail and weighs 7 ounces (200 g). This marmoset has left gouge marks in the trunk where it has been drinking gum.

7

Marmosets and tamarins, like the cotton-top tamarin seen here, were once used to test cures for human diseases.

family also helps to catch and gather food to feed the babies. Soon they are old enough to look after themselves and travel with the family through the treetops. The family group may travel through a mile (about 2 km) of forest a day, which is about one third of its home area. While the adults look for food, the young monkeys spend most of their time chasing one another and wrestling.

Marmosets and tamarins have long, soft, silky hair, and many of them have bright bushy tufts, manes, crests, and moustaches. Their appearance is often what gives these monkeys their names. For example, the cotton-top tamarin has a bushy mop of white hair on its head. The emperor tamarin has long moustaches that reminded the people that named it of those worn by the German emperor of the time.

One distinctive group of tamarins are the brightly colored lion tamarins. There are four species: the golden lion tamarin, the golden-headed lion tamarin, the black lion tamarin, and the black-headed lion tamarin.

Lion tamarins are the largest tamarins, although even they are only 31 inches (79 cm) from the top of their head to the tip of their tail and weigh 25 ounces (710 g) at the most. Like other marmosets and tamarins, lion tamarin family groups occupy an area known as a **territory**. If any lion tamarin outside the family group enters the territory,

An emperor tamarin searching for food. People used to hunt marmosets and tamarins because they were wrongly thought to carry diseases, such as yellow fever and malaria.

Areas where lion tamarins can be found

the adult monkeys in the group can be very aggressive. They will frighten the intruder away by calling loudly, chasing it, or showing off their manes.

Besides being the largest tamarins, the lion tamarins are also the rarest. All four species live in the Atlantic forest on Brazil's eastern coast. Sadly almost none of this forest is left now. It has been cut down for timber, for farmland, and to allow the area's huge cities, such as São Paulo and Rio de Janeiro, to grow. There may be fewer than 200 black lion tamarins left in the wild. Scientists think they may be among the most endangered animals in the world.

Lion tamarins can be told apart by the color of their fur. The golden lion tamarin is the only one that is completely golden all over its body.

Many of the surviving lion tamarins live in **reserves** and in state and national parks. Also, **conservationists** have set up programs to help lion tamarins. Golden lion tamarins, for example, have been bred in **captivity** and released into reserves. The future for them now looks fairly good.

Similar programs have been started for golden-headed and black lion tamarins. Only time will tell if they are going to be successful. Meanwhile, scientists are studying the black-headed lion tamarin, which lives only on the island of Superagui, near São Paulo. It seems impossible, but until 1990 no one knew this monkey existed!

Another small monkey that is losing its habitat at a fast rate is Goeldi's monkey. Goeldi's is very closely related to the marmosets and tamarins and is a small, shy monkey with a tiny face and a snub nose. Its coat may be black or

A golden-headed lion tamarin in its forest home, looking just like a tiny lion. After a day's foraging, lion tamarins sleep in tree holes or tangles of creepers, where they are safe from snakes and wild cats.

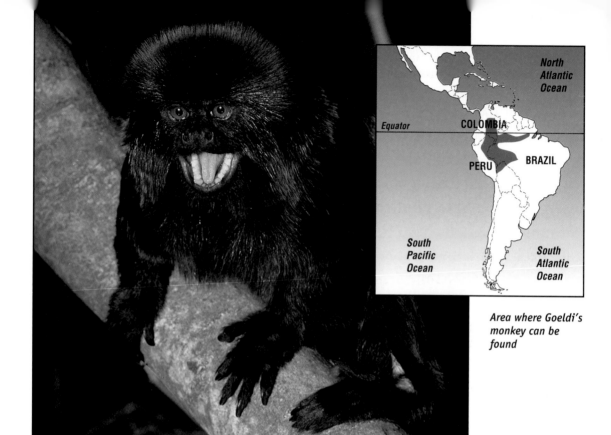

Area where Goeldi's monkey can be found

brownish black, and it has a mane around its neck and small tufts of fur on the back of its head. It is up to 25 inches (64 cm) long from its head to the tip of its tail and it weighs 24 ounces (680 g) at most.

Marmosets and tamarins usually leap noisily head first from branch to branch as they travel through the forest. Goeldi's monkeys, though, sometimes climb down to the ground, run to the next tree, and climb back up. When they do jump, Goeldi's monkeys usually leap silently from tree trunk to tree trunk, with their heads facing upward and their tails pointing down.

Some experts think that Goeldi's monkey is a marmoset; some believe it is a tamarin. Others think that it is a different kind of monkey altogether.

Another way in which Goeldi's monkeys differ from marmosets and tamarins is in the number of young they have: Goeldi's monkeys have just one baby at a time, rather than two. For the first one or two weeks, the mothers carry the little babies around on their backs, but after that the fathers and the rest of the family take charge of them.

Besides losing their forest homes, many species of marmosets and tamarins are suffering through being hunted as food and trapped as pets. There are about 20 species of marmosets and tamarins. Conservationists believe that almost all these monkeys are at risk.

A Goeldi's monkey about to eat an insect it has caught. These monkeys also eat spiders, snakes, frogs, and fruit. Goeldi's monkeys prefer to live in thick undergrowth, rather than high in the trees like most marmosets and tamarins.

Geoffroy's spider monkey
Brown-headed spider monkey
Long-haired spider monkey
Black spider monkey
Woolly spider monkey

Areas where spider monkeys can be found

Spider Monkeys

Spider monkeys are some of the largest and most apelike of the South American monkeys. Their bodies are up to 25 inches (64 cm) in length, their tails can be as long as 36 inches (91 cm), and they can weigh more than 20 pounds (9 kg). They move through the forest by swinging hand over hand below the branches. They can swing in this way because they have large, hooklike hands and extremely

It can be hard to tell one kind of spider monkey from another. This is probably a long-haired spider monkey.

long arms with flexible shoulder joints. They also have a long, grasping tail, which they can use just like an extra arm for hanging from branches or even for picking up small objects! This tail is completely bare along the underside of the tip, just like a long, sensitive finger. The bare skin has ridges to help the tail grip more firmly.

Spider monkeys live in large groups of more than 20, although these bands often split into smaller subgroups. If intruders, such as people, enter a group's territory, the monkeys make loud "barking" noises just like small terriers. They also shake the branches with their hands and feet while hanging by their tails. Sometimes they even break off twigs and drop them onto their enemies below.

Black spider monkeys on the move. Spider monkeys spend about half their day resting and the other half foraging. The animal on the right is drinking from a flower.

Spider Monkeys

There are four species of true spider monkeys: the black spider monkey, the brown-headed spider monkey, Geoffroy's spider monkey, and the long-haired spider monkey. There is also the woolly spider monkey, which is not one of the true spider monkeys, although it is closely related to them and has much in common. For example, it has long arms and legs and a long, grasping tail that can support its whole weight.

The woolly spider monkey has a short, thick coat that may be pale gray or brown. In adult males it may even be a yellowish color. Also known as the muriqui, this monkey lives in the moist Atlantic forests of eastern Brazil. At

A young spider monkey – probably a Geoffroy's – rides on its mother's tail as she climbs a tree. Spider monkeys may regularly cover about half a mile (1 km) a day in search of ripe fruit. They also eat wood, bark, leaves, and buds.

night, woolly spider monkeys gather to sleep in large groups of about 10 to 20. During the day these groups split into smaller subgroups as the monkeys set off to forage for fruit, leaves, and flowers high up in the treetops.

Woolly spider monkeys are among the most endangered of South American monkeys. As we have seen, only a tiny part of these monkeys' Atlantic forest home is left. What was once forest has been turned into cities and farmland.

The surviving woolly spider monkeys are scattered over their **range** in small numbers, and their future does not look safe. It is likely that more trees will be cut down. Added to this, people have hunted this monkey for food for hundreds of years. They still do today, even though the monkey has been protected since 1967. The four species of true spider monkeys are also threatened with becoming extinct for exactly the same reasons.

Scientists believe there may have been 400,000 woolly spider monkeys before European settlers arrived in South America. Now there are only 400 at most.

Areas where the bald uakari (red) and the black uakari (brown) can be found

Uakaris

Uakaris (wa-KA-rees) are medium-sized monkeys that measure up to 19 inches (48 cm) long, not including their short, 6-inch tail. They are the only South American monkeys to have such short tails. Males weigh about 9 pounds (4.1 kg), and the females about 8 pounds (3.6 kg).

There are two species of uakaris – the bald uakari and the black uakari. They look very different from each other. The bald uakari has a very distinctive appearance, with its bright pink or even scarlet face. As its name suggests, the bald uakari has very little hair on its head, although it does have a beard and long, shaggy hair all over its body, including its tail. This thick fur coat, which can make this monkey appear bigger than it really is, may be white, a dull

Some bald uakaris have very red faces. Others have faces that are a much paler red. Scientists think that the more sunshine a uakari gets, the redder its face becomes.

brown color, or a warm golden red. Some scientists think these different colors prove there are two kinds of bald uakari, the white and the red.

The black uakari has a black face and coat, with dark brown or reddish brown fur on its hind legs and tail. Sometimes the tail fur has yellow in it. Unlike the bald uakari, the black uakari has fur all over its head and down to its forehead.

The bald uakari lives in lowland swampy forests around the Amazon River on the border between Brazil and Peru.

A bald uakari clambers around high up in the trees. Uakaris' tails are too short and weak to hold onto branches, so these monkeys can use only their hands and feet for climbing.

A red-coated bald uakari flies through the air as it leaps from one tree to the next. Many South American monkeys are good jumpers, but uakaris are among the best of all.

For much of the year, the forests are flooded, and the bald uakari has to stay high in the trees without climbing down to the ground at all. The black uakari is found farther north than its bald cousin. It lives in the wet tropical forests of northwestern Brazil.

Uakaris are active during the day, when groups of up to 30 monkeys forage together for food. Uakari groups are usually made up of several adult males and many adult females with their young. They eat mostly fruit, but will also search out leaves, seeds, insects, and small animals such as bats and mice. Uakaris drink by dipping their hands in water and sucking their long hair. During the rainy season, when there is plenty of fruit available, uakaris share fruit trees with other monkeys, such as squirrel monkeys.

Because they live in swampy forests, uakaris are not threatened by many land animals. But they always have to be on the lookout for powerful harpy eagles, which might swoop down and snatch them from the trees. The biggest threat to uakaris, though, comes from people. The monkeys' habitat has so far been left largely untouched, but hunting is a problem. Local people have killed uakaris for many years to eat their meat. They still hunt them even though it is now against the law. Some black uakaris live in the La Macarena National Park. Sadly, though, no bald uakaris live in reserves or parks.

A black uakari takes a rest on a branch. The hair on its head makes the black uakari look very different from its bald cousin.

Areas where the common squirrel monkey (brown) and the Central American squirrel monkey (red) can be found

Squirrel Monkeys

Squirrel monkeys are small, playful monkeys. They are easy to recognize because of their distinctive markings. Their short fur is mostly yellowish brown on their back and paler yellow to white on their legs and belly. They have white, tufty, pointed ears, a white "mask" around the eyes, and a very long tail that can measure as much as 18 inches (46 cm). Male squirrel monkeys are usually larger than females, up to 15 inches (38 cm) long – not including the tail. They weigh only about 2.5 pounds (1.1 kg); females weigh about 1 pound (450 g) less.

Squirrel monkeys are extremely curious. In the wild, they sometimes sit and watch people who come into their part of the forest.

Common squirrel monkeys are found in moist forests in South America, while those of Central America are home to the Central American squirrel monkey. Squirrel monkeys generally live in large groups of 20 to 40. In some areas, such as the Amazon rainforest, they may even gather in the hundreds. No other primates, except for human beings, form such large groups. Squirrel monkey groups are made up of a large number of females and their young, along with a few adult males. The females seem to be able to get along without arguing, whereas among the males, the strong ones boss the weaker ones around, and squabbles and fights often break out over who is in charge.

The most spectacular quarrels take place in the breeding season. Just before it is time to breed, the males put on so

A common squirrel monkey perched beside the huge trunk of a rainforest tree. Squirrel monkeys can produce a nasty-smelling scent, which scientists think may help to keep enemies away.

much fat that they often become one fifth heavier than they usually are. (That's like a 70-pound child suddenly gaining 14 pounds.) Then the fights start to see which males will **mate** with the females. These brawls can be so long and hard that afterward the monkeys have to lay up and rest for a few days before they can carry on with their lives.

Since squirrel monkeys' most important food is usually fruit, female squirrel monkeys always give birth in the wet season when there is plenty of fruit available. Each female has one baby, which she carries on her back for the first month of its life. Soon the inquisitive youngster is old enough to get off and explore on its own. It learns all the information and skills it will need later in life by playing with other young squirrel monkeys. They chase each other through the trees, scream at other group members, and generally make nuisances of themselves.

A Central American squirrel monkey leaps across a gap in the trees with her baby clinging to her back. Squirrel monkeys often jump from tree to tree without even looking where they are going.

A common squirrel monkey snatches a flying insect out of the air as it buzzes past. Insects and spiders are important foods for squirrel monkeys.

Squirrel monkeys are still quite widespread in South America, but they are in serious danger in Central America. They are losing their homes and food supplies very quickly as people cut down the rainforests. To make matters worse, in the past many squirrel monkeys have been captured and sold as pets or laboratory animals around the world. To stop this from happening, the Central American squirrel monkey was added to the CITES list. CITES – the Convention on International Trade in Endangered Species – is an international agreement in which many countries say they will not buy and sell the animals on the list. This has helped, but smuggling still goes on. It is believed that less than 5000 wild squirrel monkeys remain in Central America.

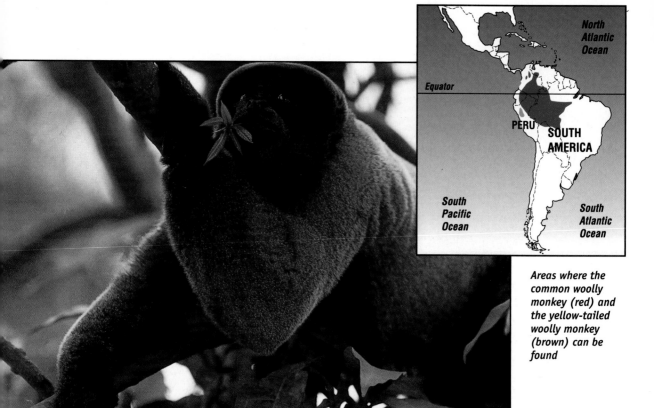

Areas where the common woolly monkey (red) and the yellow-tailed woolly monkey (brown) can be found

Woolly Monkeys

Two species of woolly monkeys exist: the common and the yellow-tailed. The range of the common woolly monkey covers much of northwestern South America, whereas the yellow-tailed is found only in Peru. It is so rare that scientists thought it had become extinct, until in 1974 they discovered one being kept as a pet by a Peruvian soldier. Since then, others have been spotted in the wild.

Woolly monkeys spend most of their time high in the trees and are often heard before they are seen. Groups of

Like its cousin the yellow-tailed, the common woolly monkey is heavy-set but gentle and gets its name from its soft fur coat.

up to 50 hurtle through the forest, snapping twigs and rustling leaves as they go. Branches shake and bounce as powerful bodies swing from beneath them or run along them with arms outstretched for balance. When they come to a gap in the trees, woolly monkeys do not hesitate to plunge off the edge into the low trees and bushes far below, then climb up the next tree and continue on their way.

Woolly monkeys eat leaves, fruit, and flowers and sometimes unroll leaves to get at insects hiding inside. They feed while it is cool, spending the hot, midday hours dozing and **grooming**. The monkeys groom one another,

Common woolly monkeys measure up to 4 feet 4 inches (1.3 m) long, including their strong, grasping tail, and weigh up to 14 pounds (6.5 kg).

Hunters often shot female woolly monkeys carrying babies as they moved through the trees high above the ground. The mother could then be eaten. The baby could be sold as a pet – if it survived the fall from the treetops.

combing through the coat to clear away dirt, insects, and knots of fur. Not only does this keep the animals' coats clean, it also strengthens the relationships among the monkeys. Woolly monkeys are affectionate toward others in the group and greet one another with a hug or a kiss.

Both species of woolly monkeys are in danger. They like to live in old rainforest. When this is cut down for timber they cannot adapt to living in the new trees that grow in its place. Woolly monkeys have also been widely hunted for food and for the pet trade. Hunting them is now against the law, but **poaching** still goes on. Since destruction of the monkeys' forest habitat also continues, the future for woolly monkeys does not look bright.

South American monkeys face many threats, but the biggest is the cutting down of their forest habitat. Since the countries in which it is happening need space for farms and cities and money from selling the timber, the destruction is unlikely to stop soon. For this reason, large areas of forest need to be turned into permanent reserves. These must be big enough to hold large numbers of animals and well enough protected to keep out poachers. Otherwise, many kinds of South American monkeys may disappear forever.

Like a tiny person, a three-month-old long-haired spider monkey peers out from behind a leaf. Action is needed if South American monkeys like this one are to have a future in the wild.

Useful Addresses

For more information about South American monkeys and how you can help protect them, contact these organizations:

Golden Lion Tamarin Management Committee
National Zoological Park
Department of Zoological Resources
3000 Connecticut Avenue NW
Washington, D.C. 20008

International Primate Protection League
Box 766
Summerville, SC 29484

U.S. Fish and Wildlife Service
Endangered Species and Habitat Conservation
400 Arlington Square
18th and C Streets NW
Washington, D.C. 20240

The Wildlife Conservation Society
185th Street and Southern Boulevard
Bronx, New York 10460

Wildlife Preservation Trust Canada
56 The Esplanade, Ste 205
Toronto ON M5E 1A7

Wildlife Preservation Trust International
3400 Girard Avenue
Philadelphia, PA 19104

World Wildlife Fund
1250 24th Street NW
Washington, D.C. 20037

Further Reading

Endangered Wildlife of the World (New York: Marshall Cavendish Corporation, 1993)

Macmillan Children's Guide to Endangered Animals Roger Few (New York: Macmillan, 1993)

Meet the Monkeys Martha Allen (Englewood Cliffs, NJ: Prentice-Hall, 1979)

Monkeys and Apes Ian Redmond (New York: Mallard Press, 1990)

Primates: Apes, Monkeys, Prosimians Thane Maynard (New York: Franklin Watts, 1994)

Wildlife at Risk: Monkeys Tess Lemmon (New York: Bookwright Press, 1992)

Wildlife of the World (New York: Marshall Cavendish Corporation, 1994)

Glossary

Adapt: To change in order to survive in new conditions.

Captivity: Confinement; for animals, usually in a cage.

Conservationist (Kon-ser-VAY-shun-ist): A person who protects and preserves the Earth's natural resources, such as animals, plants, and soil.

Extinct (Ex-TINKT): No longer living anywhere in the world.

Forage: To search for food.

Groom: To search an animal's coat and remove any insects, dirt, or knots of fur.

Gum: A sticky liquid present inside tree trunks.

Habitat: The place where an animal lives. For example, the bald uakari's habitat is the rainforest.

Mammal: A kind of animal that is warm-blooded and has a backbone. Most are covered with fur or have hair. Females have glands that produce milk to feed their young.

Mate: When a male and female get together to produce young.

Poaching: Illegal hunting.

Prey: An animal that is hunted and eaten by another animal.

Primate: A kind of mammal with human-like hands, eyes that face the front, and a well-developed brain. For example, monkeys and human beings.

Rainforest: A forest that has heavy rainfall much of the year.

Range: The area in the world in which a particular species of animal can be found.

Reserve: Land that has been set aside where plants and animals can live without being harmed.

Species: A kind of animal or plant. For example, the bald uakari is a species of monkey.

Territory: The piece of land in which a group of animals lives. Some species of monkeys defend their territory against others of their own kind.

Tropical: Having to do with or found in the tropics, the warm region of the Earth near the Equator.

Index